DATA ANALYSIS

COLORING BOOK

THIS BOOK BELONGS TO

_____

_____

Thank you for purchasing this coloring book.

Being a Data Analyst can be stressful. Coloring as an activity has scientifically shown to promote mindfuless and reduce stress. So, enjoy mindfulness and relaxation with this brilliant anti-stress therapy.

Color Test Page

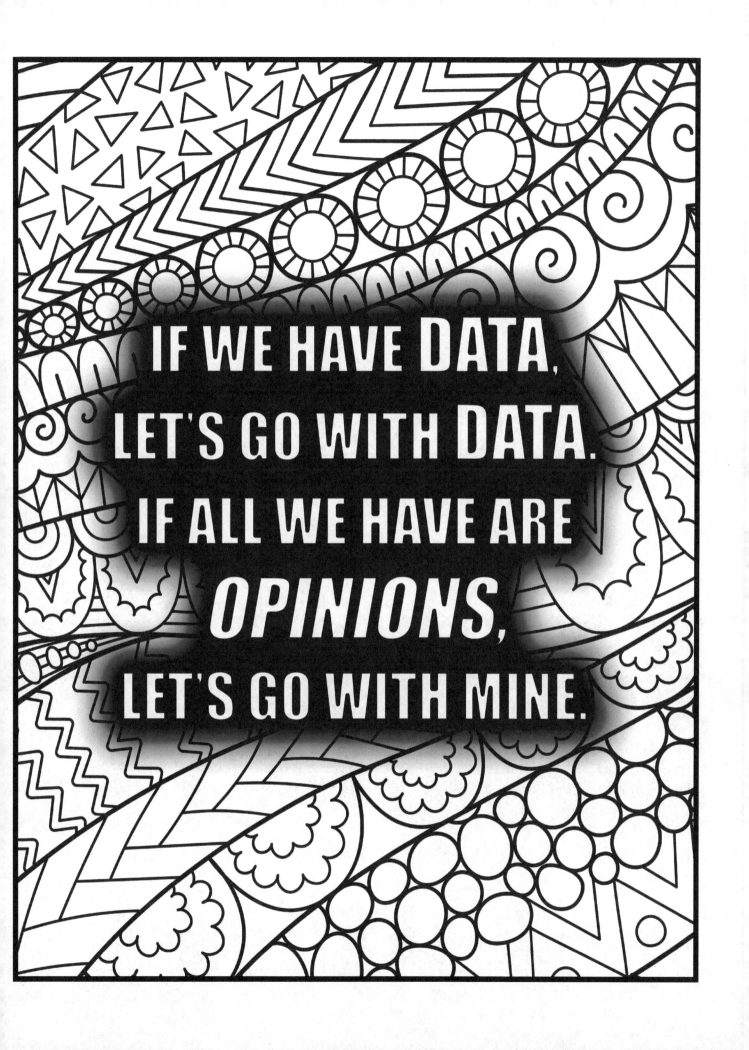

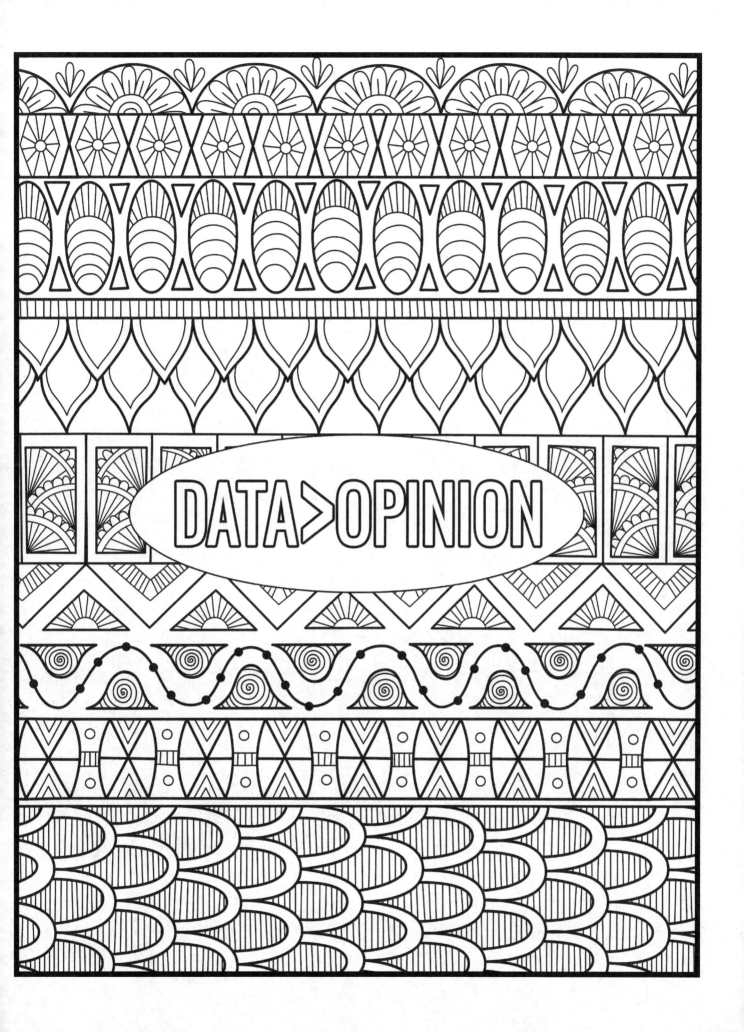

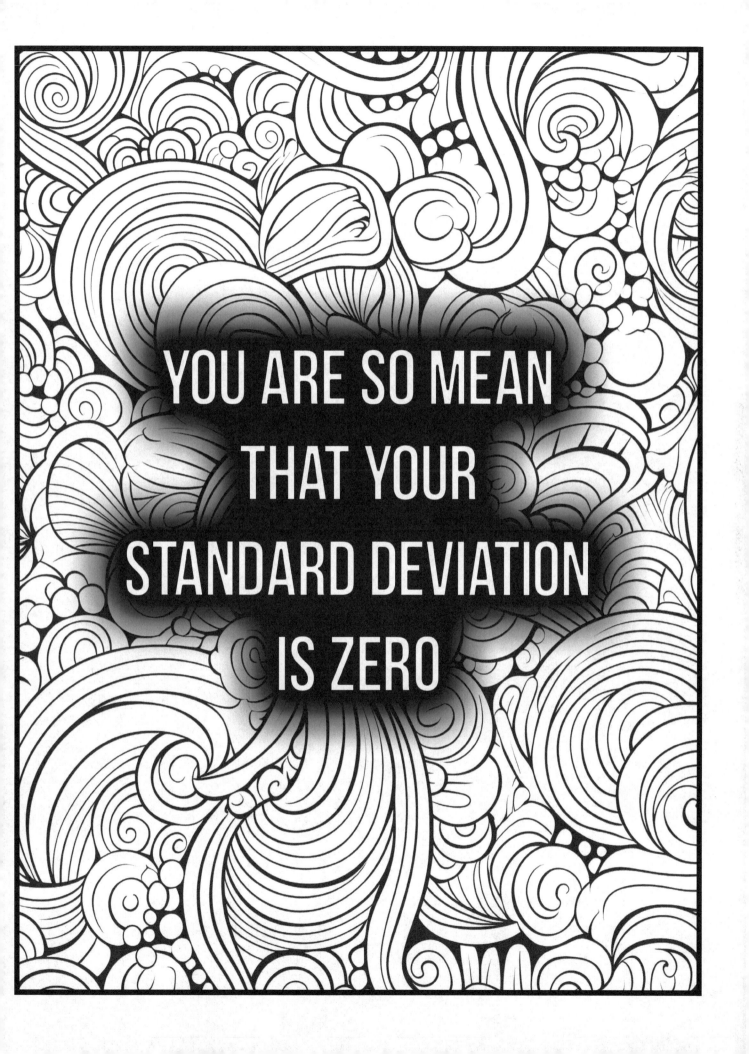

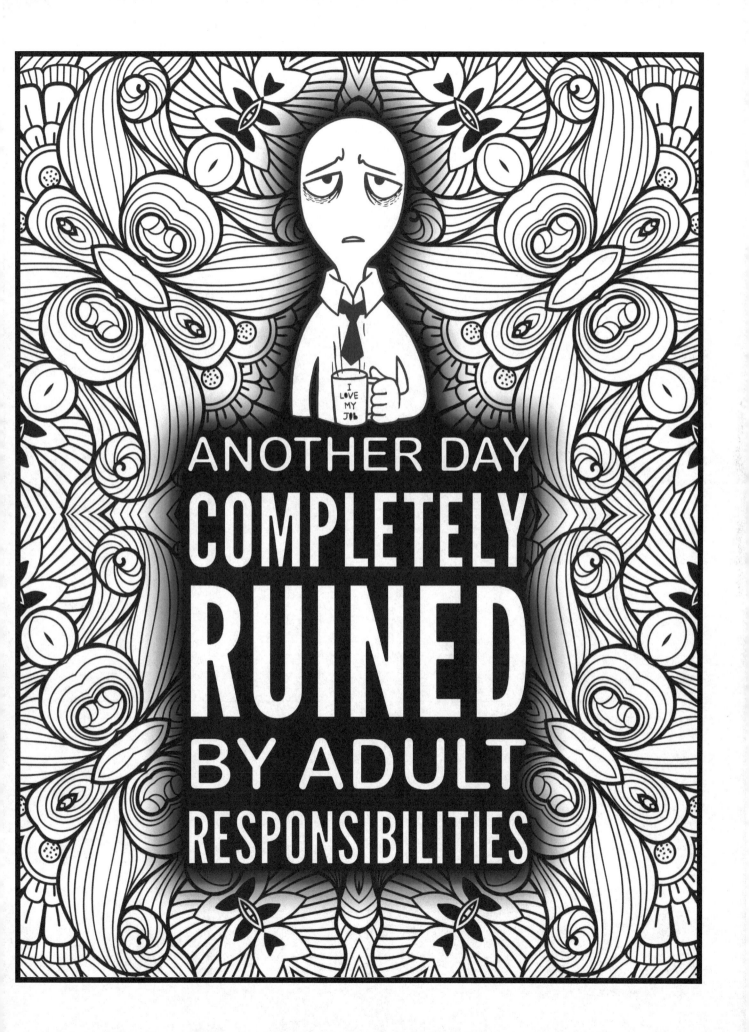

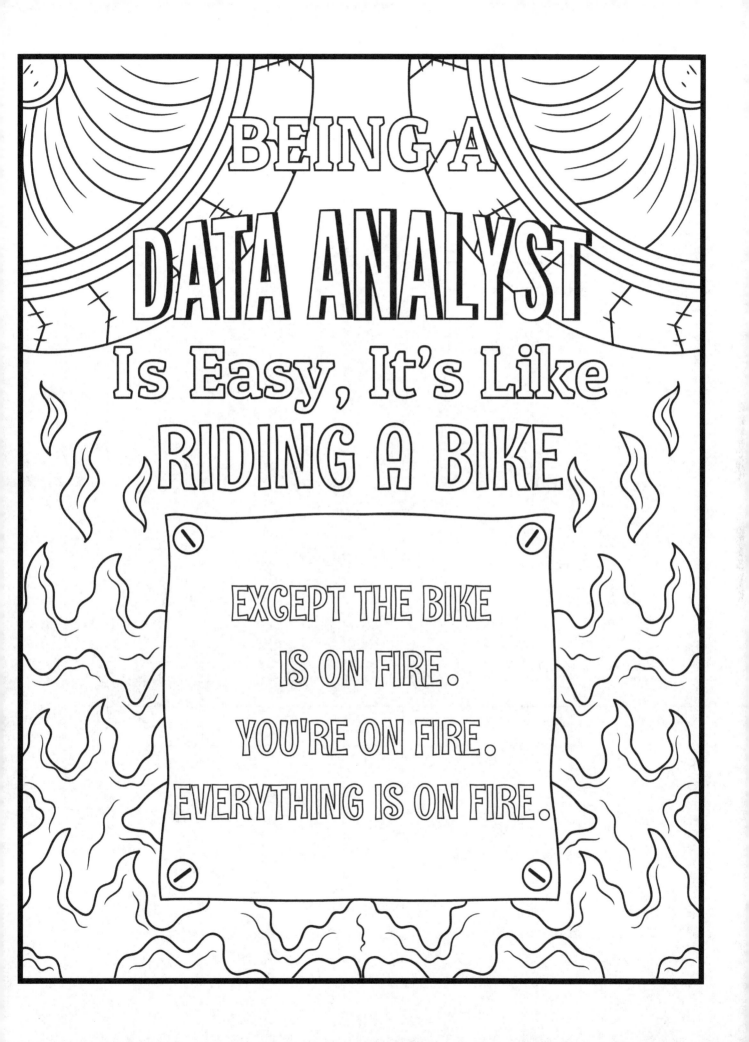

DATA ANALYST LLAMA

AIN'T GOT TIME FOR YOUR DRAMA

Made in United States
Troutdale, OR
10/30/2024

24313742R00031